Bibliographic information published by the German National Library:

The German National Library lists this publication in the National Bibliography; detailed bibliographic data are available on the Internet at http://dnb.dnb.de .

Imprint:

Copyright © 2015 GRIN Verlag
Print and binding: Books on Demand GmbH, Norderstedt Germany
ISBN: 9783668619531

This book at GRIN:

https://www.grin.com/document/300977

B. Rengeswaran, A.M. Natarajan, K. Premalatha

A Nature Inspired Algorithm for Biclustering Microarray Data Analysis

GRIN Verlag

GRIN - Your knowledge has value

Since its foundation in 1998, GRIN has specialized in publishing academic texts by students, college teachers and other academics as e-book and printed book. The website www.grin.com is an ideal platform for presenting term papers, final papers, scientific essays, dissertations and specialist books.

Visit us on the internet:

http://www.grin.com/

http://www.facebook.com/grincom

http://www.twitter.com/grin_com

Biclustering of Expression Data with Heuristic Approach

Authors:

R. Balamurugan is currently working as a Senior Research Fellow for the DBT sponsored project at Bannari Amman Institute of Technology, Erode, Tamil Nadu, India. He received his M.E. (Computer Science and Engineering) from Anna University, Chennai and B.E. (Computer Science and Engineering) from Anna University, Chennai. His areas of interest include data mining and meta-heuristic optimization techniques.

A.M. Natarajan is currently working as Chief Executive at Bannari Amman Institute of Technology, Erode, Tamil Nadu, India. He received B.E. degree, M.Sc. degree and Ph.D. from the P S G College of Technology, Coimbatore, India. He has more than 40 years of experience in Academic-Teaching, Research and Administration. He had published more than 90 papers in National and International Journals and He authored and published 10 Books. His research areas of interest include image processing, data mining and soft computing.

K. Premalatha is currently working as a Professor in the Department of Computer Science and Engineering at Bannari Amman Institute of Technology, Erode, Tamil Nadu, India. She completed her Ph. D. in Computer Science and Engineering (CSE) at Anna University, Chennai, India. She did her Master of Engineering and Bachelor of Engineering in CSE at Bharathiar University, Coimbatore, Tamil Nadu, India. Her research interests include data mining, image processing, information retrieval.

TABLE OF CONTENTS

CHAPTER   TITLE

NO.

ABSTRACT

LIST OF TABLES

LIST OF FIGURES

1   INTRODUCTION

1.1   MICROARRAY TECHNOLOGY

1.2   MICROARRAY DATA CLUSTERING ANALYSIS

1.3   BICLUSTERING

        1.3.1   Bicluster Types

1.4   MOTIVATION

1.5   PROBLEM STATEMENT

1.6   RESEARCH OBJECTIVE

1.7   ENCODING OF BICLUSTER

1.8   DATASETS USED

1.9   BIOLOGICAL VALIDATION OF BICLUSTERS

2   LITERATURE REVIEW

2.1   SYSTEMATIC BICLUSTERING ALGORITHMS

        2.1.1   Divide and Conquer Approach

        2.1.2   Greedy Iterative Search Approach

        2.1.3   Biclusters Enumeration Approach

2.2   STOCHASTIC BICLUSTERING ALGORITHMS

        2.2.1   Neighbourhood Search Approach

        2.2.2   Evolutionary Computation Approach

3   BICLUSTERING GENE EXPRESSION DATA USING

CUCKOO SEARCH

3.1   CUCKOO SEARCH

3.2   EXPERIMENT RESULTS ANALYSIS

    3.2.1   Experimental Setup

    3.2.2   Bicluster extraction for Yeast and Human Lymphoma Dataset

    3.2.3   Biological Relevance

    3.2.4   Biological Annotation for Yeast cell cycle using GOTermFinder Toolbox

3.3   SAMMARY

REFERENCES

ABSTRACT

Extracting meaningful information from gene expression data poses a great challenge to the community of researchers in the field of computation as well as to biologists. It is possible to determine the behavioral patterns of genes such as nature of their interaction, similarity of their behavior and so on, through the analysis of gene expression data. If two different genes show similar expression patterns across the samples, this suggests a common pattern of regulation or relationship between their functions. These patterns have huge significance and application in bioinformatics and clinical research such as drug discovery, treatment planning, accurate diagnosis, prognosis, protein network analysis and so on.

In order to identify various patterns from gene expression data, data mining techniques are essential. Major data mining techniques which can be applied for the analysis of gene expression data include clustering, classification, association rule mining etc. Clustering is an important data mining technique for the analysis of gene expression data. However clustering has some disadvantages. To overcome the problems associated with clustering, biclustering is introduced. Clustering is a global model where as biclustering is a local model. Discovering such local expression patterns is essential for identifying many genetic pathways that are not apparent otherwise. It is therefore necessary to move beyond the clustering paradigm towards developing approaches which are capable of discovering local patterns in gene expression data.

Biclustering is a two dimensional clustering problem where we group the genes and samples simultaneously. It has a great potential in detecting marker genes that are associated with certain tissues or diseases. However, since the problem is NP-hard, there has been a lot of research in biclustering involving statistical and graph-theoretic. The proposed Cuckoo Search (CS) method finds the significant biclusters in large expression data. The experiment results are demonstrated on benchmark datasets. Also, this work determines the biological relevance of the biclusters with Gene Ontology in terms of function.

i

LIST OF TABLES

TABLE NO.   **TITLE**

3.1   Parameter and its value

3.2   Experiment results for yeast cell expression data

3.3   Experiment results for human lymphoma expression data

3.4   Significant GO terms for three biclusters on yeast cell data

LIST OF FIGURES

FIGURE NO.   **TITLE**

1.1   Microarray Analysis

1.2   Gene expression matrix

1.3   Types of microarray clusters

1.4   Representation of vertex and its mapping to Bicluster

3.1   Fitness of the bicluster on Yeast cell-cycle data

3.2   Fitness of the bicluster on Lymphoma data

3.3   Gene expression profile of the largest bicluster on yeast
           cell-cycle data

3.4   Gene expression profile of the largest bicluster on
           Lymphoma data

3.5   Proportions of biclusters significantly enriched by GO
           annotations on yeast cell-cycle.

3.6   Gene Ontology biological functions of yeast cell cycle
           data with (20 genes)

CHAPTER 1

INTRODUCTION

Bioinformatics is an interdisciplinary subject involving fields as diverse as Biology, Statistics, Computer Science, Mathematics, Physics and Information Technology. It deals with different kinds of biological data. Microarray Gene expression data is one among them. The dimension and complexity of raw gene expression data is create challenging data analysis and data management problems. The fundamental goal of microarray gene expression data analysis is to identify the behavioral patterns of genes. An overview of Microarray Technology, Biclustering, problem formulation and the need of biological validation are discussed in this chapter.

1.1. MICROARRAY TECHNOLOGY

Cells are the basic building blocks of every organism. There is a central core in the cell called nucleus. Inside the nucleus there is an important molecule known as Deoxyribonucleic Acid (DNA). All living organisms contain DNA. A gene is a segment of DNA, which contains the formula for the chemical composition of one particular protein. Gene expression is the process of transcribing a gene's DNA sequence into Messenger Ribonucleic Acid (mRNA) sequences, which in turn are later translated into proteins. Several microarray technologies have been developed to study gene expression regulation. A most popular microarray technology is based on oligonucleotide chips. The other broadly used microarray technology is complementary DNA (cDNA)-arrays. DNA microarray technology is attracting wonderful interest in both the scientific community and in industry. Because of its ability to measure simultaneously the activities and interactions of thousands of genes (Lockhart & Winzeler 2000). A summary of the whole process of the microarray analysis can be seen in Figure 1.1.

1

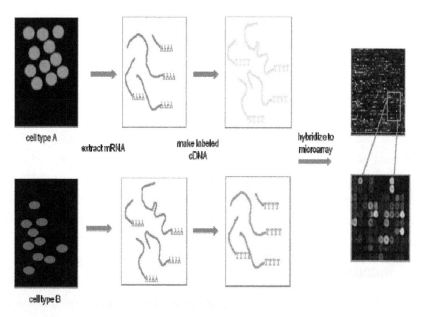

Figure 1.1 Microarray Analysis

Molecular Biology research evolves through the development of the technologies used for carrying them out. Since it is not possible to research on a large number of genes using traditional methods, DNA microarray enables the researchers to analyze the expression of many genes in a single reaction quickly and in an efficient manner. A typical DNA microarray analysis involves a multistep procedure: fabrication of microarrays by fixing properly designed oligonucleotides representing specific genes; hybridization of cDNA populations onto the microarray; scanning hybridization signals and image analysis; transformation and normalization of data; and analyzing data to identify differentially expressed genes as well as sets of genes that are co regulated.

The gene expression matrix is a processed data after the normalization procedure. Each row in the matrix corresponds to a particular gene and each column could either correspond to an experimental condition or a specific time point at which expression of the genes has been measured. The expression levels for a gene across different experimental conditions are cumulatively called the gene expression profile, and the expression levels for all genes under an experimental condition are cumulatively called the sample expression profile. An expression profile (of a gene or a sample) can be thought of as a vector and can be represented in vector space. For example, an expression profile of a gene can be considered as a vector in n dimensional space where n is the number of conditions, and an expression profile of a sample with m genes can be considered as a vector in m dimensional space where m is the number of genes). In the figure given below, the gene expression matrix X with m genes across n conditions is considered to be an m x n matrix. Each element x_i of this matrix represents the expression level of a gene under a specific condition, and is represented by a real number. Usually, it is the logarithm of the relative profusion of the mRNA of the gene under the specific condition. Figure 1.2 shows the gene expression data matrix.

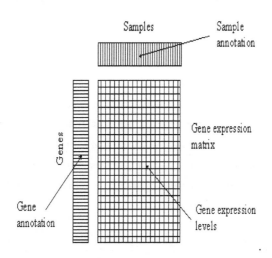

Figure 1.2 Gene expression data matrix © Mark Reimers/Exploratory Analysis

1.2   MICROARRAY DATA CLUSTERING ANALYSIS

Data mining techniques are essential in order to identify various patterns from gene expression data. Major data mining approaches which can be applied for the analysis of gene expression data include association rule mining, classification, clustering etc. Cluster analysis is an important technique to partition objects that have many attributes (multi-dimensional data) into meaningful disjoint sub-groups. Clustering process groups together similar objects into clusters. The

3

objects in each cluster are more similar to each other in the values of their attributes, than they are to objects in other groups. Clustering analysis has been extensively applied to microarray data. The goal is to extract information on how gene expression levels vary among the different samples, including groups of co-expressed genes. If two different genes show similar expression profile across the samples, this suggests a common pattern of regulation, possibly reflecting some kind of interaction or relationship between their functions (Pollard & Van Der Laan 2002). Clustering gene expression data can be categorised into the three groups, 1) gene-based, 2) sample-based and 3) subspace clustering shown in figure 1.3.

The gene-based clustering intends to group together co-expressed genes which indicate co-function, co-regulation and reveals the natural data structures. Genes are treated as the object, while the samples are the features. Clustering algorithms for gene expression data should be competent of extracting useful information from a high level of background noise. To find the substructure of the sample, regards the samples as the objects and the genes as the features. Samples are generally related to various disease or drug effects within a gene expression matrix. Therefore to identify informative genes and reduction of gene dimensionality for clustering samples to detect their substructure particular methods should be applied. To find subset of objects such that the objects emerge as a cluster in a subspace created by a subset of the feature. Biclustering, block clustering, co-clustering, subspace clustering or two-mode clustering is a technique which allows simultaneous clustering of the rows and columns of a matrix.

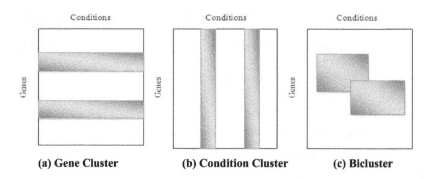

(a) Gene Cluster   (b) Condition Cluster   (c) Bicluster

Figure 1.3 Types of microarray clusters

4

1.3   BICLUSTERING

For microarray data analysis, clustering techniques is a popular technique for mining significant biological models. Clustering can support the identification of existing underlying relationships among a set of variables such as biological conditions or perturbations. Several clustering methods have been proposed for expression analysis. However, conventional clustering approaches (gene and condition based cluster) such as hierarchical, self organizing maps and k-means clustering groups the genes over all the conditions, whereas cellular processes are active only under a subset of conditions. Also, a single gene may belong to more than one group, as a gene may be involved in more than one biological process. Therefore, biclustering algorithms have been furnished as another approach to standard clustering techniques to identify local patterns from gene expression data sets. Biclustering is a two dimensional clustering problem where the genes and samples are grouped simultaneously. Biclustering also refers to the "simultaneous clustering" of both rows and columns of a data matrix. A bicluster is a subset of genes which show a similar expression profile under a subset of conditions. It has a great possible in finding marker genes that are associated with certain tissues or diseases.

1.3.1   Bicluster Types

Several types of biclusters have been described and categorised in the literature, depending on the pattern exhibited by the genes across the experimental conditions (Mukhopadhyay et al 2010). Madeira and Oliveira (2004) have identified four major groups of structures inside the submatrices are

1. Bicluster with constant value. A bicluster with constant values reveals subsets of genes with similar expression values within a subset of conditions. This situation may be expressed by:

$$a_{ij} = \mu$$

2. Bicluster with constant values on rows. A bicluster with constant values in the rows/columns identifies a subset of genes/conditions with similar expression levels across a subset of

5

conditions/genes. Expression levels might therefore vary from genes to genes or from condition to condition. It can also be expressed either in an additive or multiplicative way:

$$a_{ij} = \mu + \alpha_j \quad \text{or} \quad a_{ij} = \mu * \alpha_j$$

3. Bicluster with constant values on columns. A bicluster with constant values in the columns identifies a subset of genes/conditions with similar expression levels across a subset of conditions/genes. Expression levels might therefore vary from genes to genes or from condition to condition. It can also be expressed either in an additive or multiplicative way:

$$a_{ij} = \mu + \beta_j \quad \text{or} \quad a_{ij} = \mu * \beta_j$$

4. Bicluster with coherent values. This kind of biclusters identifies more complex relations between genes and conditions, either in an additive or multiplicative way:

$$a_{ij} = \mu + \alpha_i + \beta_j \quad \text{or} \quad a_{ij} = \mu * \alpha_i * \beta_j$$

1.4 MOTIVATION

Extracting meaningful information from gene expression data poses a great challenge to the community of researchers in the field of computation as well as to biologists. It is possible to determine the behavioral patterns of genes such as nature of their interaction, similarity of their behavior and so on through the analysis of gene expression data. Similar expression patterns are demonstrated by the genes participating in the same biological process. These patterns have vast relevance and application in bioinformatics and clinical research. These patterns are used in the medical domain for aid in more drug discovery, treatment planning, accurate diagnosis, prognosis and protein network analysis.

1.5 PROBLEM STATEMENT

Data mining techniques are essential in order to identify various patterns from gene expression data. Clustering is an important data mining approach for the analysis of gene expression data. However, there exists two main restrictions in the use of clustering algorithms: (1) genes are grouped together according to their expression patters across the whole set of samples and (2) each gene must be clustered into exactly one group. To overcome the problems associated with clustering,

6

biclustering is introduced. Let gene expression data matrix A has R rows and C columns where a cell a_{ij} is a real value that represents the expression levels of gene i under condition j. Given a matrix, biclustering finds sub-matrices, which are subgroups of genes and subgroups of conditions, where the genes exhibit highly correlated behavior for every condition. Let A_{IJ} be a submatrix of A where I $\in R$ and $J \in C$. A_{IJ} contains only the elements a_{ij} belonging to the submatrix with set of rows I and set of columns J. The residue of an element a_{ij} in a submatrix A_{IJ} equals

$$res_{i,j} = a_{i,j} + a_{I,J} - a_{I,j} - a_{i,J}$$

where a_{iJ} is the mean of the ith row in the bicluster, a_{Ij} the mean of the jth column in the bicluster, and a_{IJ} is the mean of all the elements within the bicluster. The difference between the actual value of a_{ij} and its expected value predicted from its row, column and bicluster mean are given by the residue of an element. The quality of a bicluster is evaluated by computing the Mean Square Residue (MSR), i.e. the sum of all the squared residues of its elements is given in equation (1.1):

$$f_1(I,J) = \frac{1}{|I||J|} \sum_{i \in I} \sum_{j \in J} res_{i,j}^{2} \qquad (1.1)$$

Low MSR value denotes strong coherence in the bicluster. This includes the trivial or constant bicluster where there is no fluctuation (Cheng & Church 2000). The row variance is an accompanying score to find out trivial bicluster. The row variance can be represented in equation (1.2) as follows:

$$f_2(I,J) = \frac{1}{|I|} \sum_{i \in I} v_r(i) \qquad (1.2)$$

$$v_r(i) = \frac{1}{|J|} \sum_{j \in J} (a_{i,j} - a_{i,J})^{2}$$

The fitness function for obtaining coherent biclusters is defined in equation (1.3) as follows:

$$f(I, J) = f_1(I, J) + \frac{1}{f_2(I, J)} \qquad (1.3)$$

7

to be minimized. Finding the biclusters in a microarray gene expression data is a much more complex problem than clustering. The search space for the biclustering problem is 2^{m+n} where m and n are the number of genes and conditions respectively. Usually $m+n$ is more than 2000. In fact, it has been proven to be a NP-hard problem (Tanay et al 2002).

1.6   RESEARCH OBJECTIVE

The primary objective of this thesis is:

➢ To derive the heuristic approach for the identification of coherent biclusters from gene expression data with minimum MSR and maximum row variance.

1.7   ENCODING OF BICLUSTER

Each population is represented as candidate solution for the problem. Solutions are encoded by means of binary strings of length $N+M$, where N and M are the number of rows (genes) and of columns (conditions) of the expression data. A bit is set to one if the corresponding gene and/or condition is present in the bicluster, and reset to zero otherwise. So the individual dimension of solution is represented by a real number. The mapping function of solution into a binary string representation of a bicluster is given in Equation (1.4) as follows:

$$
y_{ij} = \begin{cases} x_{ij} \geq 0.5 & 1 \\ otherwise & 0 \end{cases} \tag{1.4}
$$

Where

x_{ij} - Random value generated for j^{th} gene/condition of ith solution

y_{ij} - Binary string representation of bicluster of x_{ij}

In y_{ij}, if a bit is set to 1 then the corresponding gene or condition belongs to the encoded bicluster; otherwise it is not. Figure 1.4 shows the representation of solution and its mapped bicluster representation.

8

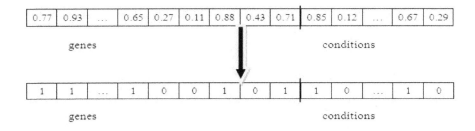

| 0.77 | 0.93 | ... | 0.65 | 0.27 | 0.11 | 0.88 | 0.43 | 0.71 | 0.85 | 0.12 | ... | 0.67 | 0.29 |

genes   conditions

| 1 | 1 | ... | 1 | 0 | 0 | 1 | 0 | 1 | 1 | 0 | ... | 1 | 0 |

genes   conditions

Figure 1.4 Representation of vertex and its mapping to Bicluster

1.8   DATASETS USED

The experiments are conducted on two well–known datasets namely Yeast and Lymphoma (Cheng & church 2000). Yeast dataset consists of 2884 genes and 17 conditions. The values in the expression dataset are integers in the range 0 to 600. The second dataset is the human B–cells expression data. Human B-cell Lymphoma expression dataset contains 4026 genes and 96 conditions. The values in the dataset are integers in the range -750 to 650.

1.9   BIOLOGICAL VALIDATION OF BICLUSTERS

Biological validation can qualitatively evaluate the capacity of an algorithm to extract meaningful biclusters from a biological point of view. Prior biological knowledge can be used to evaluate the biological significance of biclusters obtained (Tanay et al 2002). If the identified biclusters contain significant proportion of biologically similar genes, then it proves that the biclustering technique produces biologically relevant results. The biological significance can be verified using gene ontology database. The Gene Ontology (GO) project provides three structured, controlled vocabularies that describe gene products in terms of their associated biological processes, cellular components and molecular functions in a species independent manner. The tools systematically map a large number of interesting genes in a list to the associated biological annotation terms (e.g. GO Terms or Pathways), and then statistically examine the enrichment of gene members for each of the annotation terms by comparing the outcome to the control (or reference) background. The enriched annotation terms associated with the large gene list will give important insights that allow investigators to understand the biological themes behind the large gene list. The

9

degree of enrichment is measured by p-values which use a cumulative hyper geometric distribution to compute the probability of observing the number of genes from a particular GO category (function, process and component) within each bicluster. The probability p for finding at least k genes from a particular category within a cluster of size m is given in Equation (1.5).

$$p = 1 - \sum_{r=0}^{k-1} \frac{\binom{G}{r}\binom{M-G}{m-r}}{\binom{M}{m}} \qquad (1.5)$$

Where G is the total number of genes within a category and M is the total number of genes within the genome. The p-value is the probability that the genes are selected into the cluster by random. A small p-value implies that the cluster is highly differed found by chance. The annotations of genes for three ontologies including biological process, cellular component and molecular function are obtained.

CHAPTER 2

LITERATURE REVIEW

The biclustering algorithms are classified into two different approaches: systematic search algorithms and heuristic search algorithms. As it has already been mentioned, the biclustering problem is NP-hard (Tanay et al 2002). This entails that an exhaustive search of the space of solutions may be infeasible. For that reason, heuristic search algorithms are usually used to approximate the problem by finding suboptimal solutions. This chapter deals with the review of various biclustering techniques available for gene expression data analysis.

2.1   SYSTEMATIC BICLUSTERING ALGORITHMS

2.1.1   Divide and Conquer Approach

Generally, a divide and conquer approach works by recursively breaking down a problem into two or more sub-problems of the same (or related) type, until these become simple enough to be solved directly. The solutions to the sub-problems are then combined to give a solution to the original problem. With this approach, initially a bicluster representing the whole data matrix then it divides into two submatrices to obtain two biclusters. Then reiterate recursively this process until to get a certain number of biclusters verifying a specific set of properties.

The biclustering algorithm called direct clustering is proposed by Hartigan (1972) was one of the first works ever published on biclustering, although it was not applied to gene expression data. The algorithm is based on the use of a divide and conquers approach, in which the input matrix is iteratively partitioned into a set of sub-matrices, until k matrices are obtained, where k is an input parameter for the number of desired biclusters. The advantage of this approach is that it is fast, nevertheless, the main drawback of this method is that partitions cannot be reconsidered once they have been split.

The Bimax algorithm of Prelic et al. (2006) is a method for finding subgroups of 1 value in a binary matrix. All values above the threshold will be set to one, all those below to zero. The

11

discretization scheme defines if only down or up-regulated genes (or both) will be considered. The data matrix M' partition into three submatrices, one of which contains only 0-cells. The algorithm is then recursively applied to the remaining two submatrices and ends if the current matrix represents a bicluster which contains only 1's. Although being very fast, however, its biggest disadvantage is that it may ignore good biclusters by partitioning them before identifying them.

Zhao et al (2008) presented a new geometric biclustering algorithm based on the Hough Transform. Based on the linear structures in column-pair spaces and divide them into different patterns using the Additive and Multiplicative Pattern Plot (AMPP). These sub-biclusters are combined step by step to form large biclusters. Hough Transform is performed in a two-dimensional (2-D) space of column pairs. The coherent columns are then combined iteratively to form larger and larger biclusters. This reduces the computational complexity considerably and makes it possible to analyze large-scale microarray data.

Yang et al (2011) proposed a novel transform technique based on Singular Value Decomposition (SVD) to extract significant biclusters. The whole process includes three steps: The first step, based on the property of SVD, the problem of identifying correlated biclusters is transformed into two global clustering problems. The second step, the Bidirectional Mixed Clustering algorithm motivated by agglomerative hierarchical clustering is applied to discover the original biclusters which are not mutually exclusive. The last step, based on original biclusters, the inclusion-maximal biclusters are revealed by Lift algorithm. Even though extracting negative correlation gene pairs, however biggest issue is that it may ignore good biclusters by partitioning them and quality of biclusters fully depends on the more number of initial parameter value.

2.1.2   Greedy Iterative Search Approach

This approach builds a solution in a step-by-step way using a given quality measure. Decisions made at each step are based on information at hand without worrying about the effect these decisions may have in the future. Moreover, once a decision is taken, it becomes permanent and is never reconsidered. By applying this approach to the biclustering problem, at each iteration, submatrices of the data matrix are constructed by adding/removing a row/column to/from the current

12

submatrix that maximizes/minimizes a certain function. This process reiterate until no other row/column can be added/removed to/from any submatrix.

Ben-Dor et al (2003) defined a bicluster as an Order-Preserving Sub-Matrix (OPSM). This way, a sub-matrix is said to be order preserving if there is a permutation of its columns under which the sequence of values in every row is strictly increasing. This strict condition might be relaxed for real expression data, where rows having a significant tendency to be similarly ordered are searched for instead. It focuses on the coherence of the relative order of the conditions rather than the coherence of actual expression levels based on the probabilistic model. The algorithm can also be used to discover more than one bicluster in the same dataset, even when they are overlapped. However, in this model concerns only the order of values and thus makes the model quite restrictive.

An Iterative Signature Algorithm (ISA) provides a definition of biclusters as transcription modules to be retrieved from the expression data proposed by Bergmann et al (2003). It starts with a set of input seeds and the fixed points find corresponding to each seed through iterations. These distinct fixed points are collect in order to decompose the expression data into modules. The structure of this decomposition depends on the choice of thresholds. The first normalization step in ISA may cause increased overlap degree. Because the range of expression values after normalization becomes narrower with increased overlapping, the differences between normal and significant expression values blur and are more difficult to separate.

To address random masking of the values in the data matrix issue and to further accelerate the biclustering process, the authors presented a new model of bicluster to incorporate null values. Yang et al (2005) proposed an algorithm named FLexible Overlapped biclustering (FLOC) able to discover a set of k possibly overlapping biclusters simultaneously based on probabilistic moves. Bicluster volume is taken into account within the possible actions, where bigger biclusters are preferred, and the variance is used to reject constant biclusters. The whole process ends when no action that improves the overall quality can be found.

Liu & Wang (2007) proposed the Maximum Similarity Bicluster (MSB) algorithm. It starts by constructing a similarity matrix based on a reference gene. Then a process of iteratively remove the row or column in the bicluster with the worst similarity score is perform, until there is one

13

element left in the bicluster. MSB performs well for overlapping biclusters and works well for additive biclusters. But, it works for the special case of approximately squares biclusters. In order to overcome this issue, an extension algorithm named Randomized MSB Extension (RMSBE) algorithm is also presented.

DiMaggio et al (2008) presented an approach based on the Optimal RE-Ordering of the rows and columns of a data matrix so as to globally minimize dissimilarity metric. Converse to OPSM, this approach allows for monotonicity violations in the reordering, but penalize their contributions according to a selected objective function. The algorithm begins by optimally re-ordering a single dimension of the data matrix. After that, the median is computed for each pair of adjacent elements (either rows or columns), where the largest median values define the cluster boundaries between the re-ordered elements. These cluster boundaries are then used to partition the original matrix into several sub-matrices. However, the main drawback of this method is that extracts trivial solutions.

Angiulli et al (2008) presented a biclustering algorithm based on a greedy technique enriched with a local search strategy to escape poor local minima named Random Weight Biclustering (RWB) which produces one bicluster at a time. Initially it starts with random solution then it searches for a locally optimal solution by successive transformations that improve the gain functions such as MSR, gene variance and volume. A transformation is done only if there is reduction of MSR or an increase either in the gene variance or the volume. In order to avoid getting trapped into poor local minima, the algorithm executes random moves according to a probability given by the user. Moreover, degree of overlapping rate is controlled for genes and conditions independently by using two different frequency thresholds.

Li et al (2009) presented as a QUalitative BIClustering algorithm (QUBIC), in which the input data matrix is first represented as a matrix of integer values, either in a qualitative or semi-qualitative manner. The first step of the algorithm corresponds to the construction of a weighted graph from the (semi-) qualitative matrix, with genes represented as vertices, and edges connecting every pair of genes. Edge weights are computed in the base of the similarity level between the two corresponding rows. After the graph has been created, biclusters are identified one by one, starting for each bicluster with the heaviest unused edge as a seed. However it delivers approximative solutions without optimality guarantees.

14

Ayadi et al (2011) presented an algorithm BicFinder for extracting biclusters from microarray data which constructs a Directed Acyclic Graph (DAG) to combine a subset of genes under a subset of conditions iteratively, by adopting the evaluation function Average Correspondence Similarity Index. BicFinder, do not require fixing a minimum or a maximum number of genes or conditions, enabling a generation of diversified biclusters. However, it places restrictive constraints on the structure of the biclustering solutions.

2.1.3   Biclusters Enumeration Approach

This approach tries to enumerate (explicitly or implicitly) all the solutions for an original problem. The enumeration process is generally represented by a search tree. By applying this approach to the biclustering problem, identify all the possible groups of biclusters in order to keep the best one. This approach has the advantage of being able to obtain the best solutions. Its disadvantage is that it is costly in computing time and in memory space.

Tanay et al (2002) based their approach on graph theoretic coupled with statistical modeling of the data, where SAMBA stands for Statistical Algorithmic

Method for Bicluster Analysis. In their work, they framework the input expression data as a bipartite graph whose two parts correspond to conditions and genes, respectively, and edges refer to significant expression changes. Finally the significant biclusters were identified using graph theoretic approach whereas due to its high complexity, the number of rows the bicluster may have is restricted. This way, discovering the most significant biclusters means finding the heaviest sub-graphs in the model bipartite graph, where the weight of a sub-graph is the sum of the weights of the gene-condition pairs in it.

A MicroCluster algorithm is proposed by Zhao & Zaki (2005) as a biclustering method for mining maximal biclusters satisfying certain homogeneity criteria. It follows an enumeration method consisting of three steps. In the first step the multi-graph is created, a second step is applied for mining the maximal clusters from it, based on a recursive depth-first search. Although the output of this step is the final set of biclusters, a final step is optionally executed so as to delete or merge those biclusters according to several overlap conditions. This strategy succeeds in discovering shifting pattern biclusters by using exponential transformations. Even so, there is difficulty to generate scaling pattern.

15

The BiMine algorithm of Ayadi et al (2009) is a method for finding coherent bicluster relies on a new evaluation function called Average Spearman's rho (ASR). It uses a new tree structure, called Bicluster Enumeration Tree (BET), to represent the different biclusters discovered during the enumeration process. Compared to other data structure, the BET permits to represent the maximum number of significant biclusters and the links that exist between these biclusters. There is no overlapping control is carried out among the reported solutions.

Ayadi et al (2012) proposed a biclustering algorithm, called BiMine+, which is able to detect significant biclusters from gene expression data. The algorithm uses a Modified Bicluster Enumeration Tree (MBET) to represent the identified biclusters, where each node of MBET contains the gene profile shape of a bicluster. The profile shape of a gene is defined as the behavior of this gene, i.e., up, down or no change, over the conditions of the bicluster to which this gene belongs. However, this algorithm is computational time expensive.

A CoBi: Pattern Based Co-Regulated Biclustering is presented by Roy et al (2013) as a biclustering method for grouping both positively and negatively regulated genes from microarray expression data. Regulation pattern and similarity in degree of fluctuation are accounted for while computing similarity between two genes. To generate biclusters, it uses a tree-based algorithm called BiClust. An advantage of BiClust is that it requires a single pass over the database to generate all biclusters. Nevertheless, the main drawback of this method is that extracts small biclusters for large MSR value.

2.2. STOCHASTIC BICLUSTERING ALGORITHMS

2.2.1 Neighbourhood Search Approach

A neighborhood search, also called local search starts with an initial solution s and then moves iteratively to a neighboring solution. A neighboring solution is generally generated by applying a transformation operator, also called move operator, to the current solution. For instance, the basic hill-climbing strategy replaces the current solution by a neighbouring solution of better quality. By using this approach to the biclustering problem, an initial solution which can be a bicluster or the whole matrix. Then, at each iteration this solution can be improved by adding and/or removing some genes/conditions to minimize/maximize a certain function.

Cheng & Church (2000) were the first apply this concept to biclustering to gene expression data. Their goal is to find biclusters with a MSR value lower than a fixed threshold. Hence, they proposed an iterative search procedure which deletes/adds genes/conditions to the biclusters. The single node deletion method iteratively removes the gene or column that has low quality according to MSR. This strategy succeeds in discovering biclusters with coherent values, Since, the algorithm discovers one bicluster at a time, repeated application of the method on a modified matrix is needed for discovering multiple biclusters. This has the drawback that it results in highly overlapping gene sets.

Bryan et al (2006) proposed an application of simulated annealing to the biclustering of gene expression data. In this approach, the fitness of each solution is given by its MSR value, and ten times the number of genes successes needed to be achieved before cooling. This number determines the depth of the search, being a success an improvement on the fitness function. The initial temperature of the system, as well as the rate at which it is lowered are also important, since both of them determine the number of total iterations and also affect the convergence. In their work, they used the same method of Cheng & Church (2000), replacing the original values for random ones, in an attempt to prevent them to be part of any further bicluster.

The traditional Particle swarm optimization (PSO) is known to suffer from stagnation once particles have prematurely converged to any particular region of the search space. Liu et al (2009) presented their biclustering approach on the use of a PSO together with crowding distance as the nearest neighbour search strategy, which speed up the convergence to the Pareto front and also guarantee diversity of solutions. The author focus on three objectives, the size, homogeneity and row variance of biclusters, are satisfied simultaneously by applying three fitness functions in optimization framework. By using PSO has shown its fast search speed in many complicated optimization and search problems. Even so, there is difficulty to select probable value of inertia weight.

17

A similar approach to that of Cheng and Church has been followed by Mukhopadhyay et al (2009) in order to incorporate a new coherence measure called scaling mean squared residue (SMSR) into a search heuristic. While SMSR is only able to recognize multiplicative models, the authors propose and adapted algorithm in which CC is applied twice, the first time using MSR as the evaluation measure and the second time using SMSR. This allows finding biclusters with shifting patterns and also biclusters with scaling patterns, but it does not find biclusters with both kinds of patterns simultaneously.

Ayadi et al (2012) presented a Pattern Driven Neighborhood Search (PDNS) approach for the biclustering problem. PDNS first follows up a preprocessing step to transform the input data matrix to a behavior matrix and a dedicated neighborhood taking into account various patterns information. It also utilizes fast greedy algorithms to generate diversified initial biclusters of reasonable quality and a randomized perturbation strategy. The algorithm outputs one bicluster at a time. Therefore, in order to obtain several biclusters it must be run several times with different initial solutions. In this work, the authors use the output of two fast well-known algorithms as initial biclusters. Nevertheless, no overlapping control is carried out among the reported solutions.

2.2.2 Evolutionary Computation Approach

The evolutionary computation approach is based on the natural evolutionary process. An evaluation mechanism is established to assess the quality of each individual. Evolution operators eliminate some individuals and produce new individuals from selected individuals. By applying this approach to the biclustering problem, it starts from an initial population of solutions, i.e., biclusters or the whole matrix, then, the quality of each solution of the population can be measured by the fitness function. New solutions are obtained by using recombination and mutation operators. This process ends when a prefixed stop condition is verified.

Bleuler et al (2004) were the first in developing an evolutionary biclustering algorithm. They proposed the use of binary strings for the individuals representation, and an initialization of random solutions but uniformly distributed according to their sizes. Bit mutation and uniform crossover are used as reproduction operators, and a fitness function that prioritizes MSR. A diversity maintenance strategy is carried out which decreases the amount of overlapping among bicluster. However, it returns trivial bicluster.

Divina & Aguilar-Ruiz (2006) presented as a Sequential Evolutionary BIclustering approach (SEBI). The term sequential refers the way in which bicluster are discovered, being only one bicluster obtained per each run of the evolutionary algorithm. In order to obtain several biclusters, a sequential strategy is adopted, invoking several times the evolutionary process. Furthermore, a matrix of weights is used for the control of overlapped elements among the different solutions. This weight matrix is initialized with zero values and is updated every time a bicluster is returned. Even so, it works well for the special case of approximately small biclusters.

A Multi-Objective Evolutionary algorithm (MOEA) based on pareto dominance is presented by Mitra & Banka (2006). Unlike single objective optimization problems, the MOEA tries to optimize two or more conflicting characteristics represented by fitness functions. A local search strategy based on the node insertion and node deletion phases of CC algorithm is applied to all of the individuals at the beginning of every generational loop. In order to maintain diversity in the population, a measure called crowding distance is used. This approach has the advantage of being able to extract a large size of bicluster to a given threshold. However, the main drawback of this method is that converges slowly and consumes much time to find the best solutions.

Liu et al (2006) proposed a biclustering algorithm based on the use of an Estimation of Distribution Algorithms (EDAs) together with Genetic Algorithm (GA) to escape from slow convergence rate and reduce the computation time. EDAs are stochastic heuristic search strategies that form part of the evolutionary computation approaches. A number of solutions in the next generation are created by a directed acyclic graph, which is induced from the previous population. In EDAs the interrelations between the different variables representing the individuals are expressed clearly by means of the joint probability distribution associated with the selected individuals at each generation. This method can't extract find the overlapped bicluster.

Biclustering via a Hybrid Evolutionary Algorithm (BiHEA) was proposed by Gallo et al (2009) and is very similar to the evolutionary biclustering algorithm of Bleuler et al (2004). However, they differ in the crossover operator and BiHEA also integrates gene variance in the

19

fitness function. This method incorporates two mechanisms: the first one avoids loss of good solutions through generations; and the second one is elitism, in which a predefined number of best biclusters are directly passed to next generation without overlap.

Huang et al (2012) have proposed a biclustering algorithm based on the use of an Evolutionary Algorithm (EA) together with hierarchical clustering. In this method, the conditions are separated into a number of conditions subsets, also called subspaces. The evolutionary algorithm is then applied to each subspace in parallel, and an expanding and merging phase is finally employed to combine the subspaces results into the output biclusters. So it is called as Condition-Based Evolutionary Biclustering. The parallel computing technology would be of great help to speedup the traditional EA framework. But, its disadvantage is that it is extract small volume of bicluster.

Maatouk et al (2014) proposed an Evolutionary Biclustering algorithm based on the new crossover method (EBACross). It uses a fast local search algorithm to generate an initial population with better quality. The use of standard deviation to discretize the parent biclusters allows to closest expression level of each gene and to construct the variance matrix. This matrix helps to determinate the genes presenting a similar behaviour and to extract biclusters with highly correlated genes. In order to avoid overlapping biclusters and to increase the diversification biclusters a mutation operator used. However it possibly takes a very long time on large inputs.

CHAPTER 3

BICLUSTERING GENE EXPRESSION DATA USING CUCKOO SEARCH

Nature inspired metaheuristic algorithms such as Genetic Algorithm (GA), Particle Swarm Optimization (PSO), Cuckoo Search (CS) and so on, start to show their power in dealing with NP-hard problems (Yang 2010). The CS algorithm is inspired by the reproduction strategy of cuckoos. It combines the advantages of both GA and PSO. In this chapter, the algorithm named Cuckoo Search is proposed for find the coherent biclusters with minimum MSR in large expression data. An overview of CS is discussed in this chapter with experimental result analysis.

3.1 CUCKOO SEARCH

The CS is one of the metaheuristic optimization approach developed by Xin-She Yang & Suash Deb (2009) based on the brood parasitism of the cuckoo species by laying their eggs in the nests of other host bird. Based on the selfish gene theory (Dawkins 1989), this parasitic behavior increases the chance of survival of the cuckoo's genes. Since the cuckoo need not spend any energy rearing its young one. The CS algorithm utilizes these behaviors in order to traverse the search space and find optimal solutions. A set of nests with one egg are placed in random locations in the search space where the each egg represent a candidate solution. The number of cuckoos is assigned to traverse the search space, recording the highest objective values for different encountered candidate solutions. The cuckoos utilize a search pattern called Levy flight which is encountered in real insects, fish and birds. When generating new solutions $x(t+1)$ for a cuckoo i, a Levy flight is performed using the following equation (3.1)

$$x_i (t + 1) = x_i (t) + \alpha \oplus Levy(\lambda)$$
(3.1)

The symbol $\oplus$ is an entry-wise multiplication. Basically Levy flights provides a random walk while their random steps are drawn from a Levy distribution for large steps given in equation (3.2)

$$Levy \sim u = t^{-\lambda}$$
(3.2)

which has an infinite variance with an infinite mean. Here the consecutive jumps of a cuckoo essentially form a random walk process which obeys a power-law step-length distribution with a heavy tail. The rules for CS are described as follows:

- Each cuckoo lays one egg at a time, and dumps it in a randomly chosen nest
- The best nests with high quality of eggs will carry over to the next generations;
- The number of available host nests is fixed, and a host can discover a foreign egg with a probability $p_a \in [0, 1]$. In this case, the host bird can either throw the egg away or abandon the nest so as to build a completely new nest in a new location.

Algorithm 1 : *Pseudo code for Cuckoo Search with Levy flight*

Generate random population with n nests and each nest consists of an egg.

while (*t*<MaxGeneration) or (stop criterion)

Get a cuckoo randomly (say, *i*) and replace its solution by performing Levy flights;
Evaluate its fitness F_i
Choose a nest among *n* (say, *j*) randomly;

if $(F_i < F_j)$

Replace *j* by the new solution;

end if

A fraction (p_a) of the worse nests is abandoned and new ones are built;

Keep the best solutions/nests;

Rank the solutions/nests and find the current best;

Pass the current best to the next generation;

end while

Only two parameters are needed to be supplied to this algorithm, the discovery rate and the size of the population *n*. When *n* is fixed, p_a is used to control the elitism and the balance of randomization and local search. This fact not only increases the ease of implementation, but also potentially makes it a more general optimization solution to be applied to a wide range of problems.

3.2   EXPERIMENT RESULTS ANALYSIS

3.2.1   Experimental Setup

The CS presented for the bicluster problem are implemented in MATLAB and run on an Intel i3 3.7 GHz. The nest size of CS is 50. The minimum fitness value is obtained for 20 biclusters with the stopping criterion is up to the maximum iteration 1000. The parameters p_a, α and λ are set as 0.25, 1 and 1.5 respectively (Yang & Deb 2009). Table 3.1 shows the parameter and its value used in this paper.

Table 3.1. Parameter and its value

Parameter	Value
Number of biclusters	20
Number of nest	50
p_a	0.25
α	1
λ	1.5
Iterations	1000

3.2.2   Bicluster extraction for Yeast and Human Lymphoma Dataset

Granting to the problem formulation an extracted bicluster should be as satisfying a homogeneity criterion. The bicluster should satisfy two requirements simultaneously. The expression levels of each gene within the bicluster should be similar over the range of conditions. That is it should have a low MSR score. On the other hand, the bicluster row variance should be high. The MSR represents the variance of the selected genes and conditions with respect to the homogeneity of the bicluster and row variance removes the simple bicluster. To quantify biclusters homogeneity and size satisfy the Coherence Index (CI) is used as a measure for evaluating their goodness. CI is defined as the ratio of MSR score to the size of the formed bicluster. The size of a bicluster increases while CI proportionately decreases. Table 3.2 and 3.3 show the experimental result obtained for yeast cell cycle data and human lymphoma data respectively. Totally five biclusters are chosen randomly from the total number of biclusters. Figure 3.1 and 3.2 show the fitness value obtained for yeast cell cycle data and human lymphoma data respectively.

23

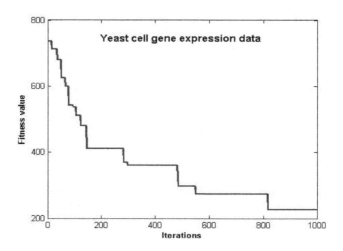

Figure 3.1. Fitness of the bicluster on Yeast cell-cycle data

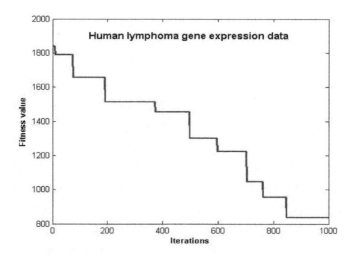

Figure 3.2. Fitness of the bicluster on Lymphoma data

Table 3.2 summarizes the best biclusters for Yeast data after 1000 generations. The largest size bicluster is found at MSR=252.12, with coherence index CI being minimal and indicating the goodness of the discovered partitions. The minimum value of CI is 0.0787 with a corresponding size

24

of 3200 being the best in the table. As mentioned earlier, a low mean squared residue indicates a high coherence of the discovered biclusters.

Table 3.2. Experiment results for yeast cell expression data

Bicluster	Genes	Conditions	Volume	MSR	Row Variance	CI
BC_1	184	8	1472	182.69	826.14	0.1241
BC_3	286	6	1716	193.63	912.26	0.1128
BC_7	327	8	2616	222.54	930.02	0.0850
BC_{18}	318	9	2862	236.26	796.63	0.0825
BC_9	320	10	3200	252.12	962.74	0.0787

Table 3.3 summarizes the best biclusters for Human B-cell data after 1000 generations. The largest sized bicluster is found at MSR=869.85, with coherence index CI being minimal and indicating the goodness of the discovered partitions. The minimum value of CI is 0.09 with a corresponding size of 9660 being the best in the table. As mentioned earlier, a low mean squared residue indicates a high coherence of the discovered biclusters.

Table 3.3. Experiment results for human lymphoma expression data

Bicluster	Genes	Conditions	Volume	MSR	Row Variance	CI
BC_1	222	28	6216	796.3	1863.23	0.1281
BC_8	254	33	8382	826.63	1986.06	0.0986
BC_9	269	32	8608	838.79	2264.22	0.0974
BC_{12}	324	27	8748	846.45	2086.13	0.09675
BC_{15}	276	35	9660	869.85	2187.37	0.0900

Figure 3.3 depicts the gene expression profile of this largest bicluster, corresponding to MSR=252.12. The gene expression values in the range 150 to 350 indicate the highly dense profiles of the co regulated genes having little or no fluctuations under the selected conditions of the bicluster. It has the highest row variance is 962.74 whereas has the MSR is 252.12. In terms of fitness, this is the most "interesting" bicluster which has largest volume 3200 with the lowest MSR.

Moreover, CS tries to find highly row-variant biclusters instead of trivial biclusters using row varience.

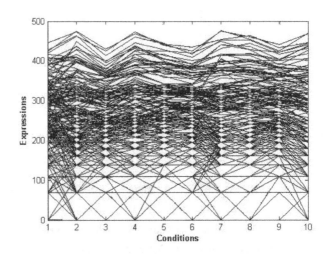

Figure 3.3. Gene expression profile of the largest bicluster on yeast cell-cycle data

Figure 3.4 depicts the gene expression profile of this largest bicluster, corresponding to minimum MSR=869.85. It has the highest row variance = 2187.37, whereas has the MSR=869.85. In terms of fitness=869.85, this is the most "interesting" bicluster which has largest volume 9660 with the lowest MSR. The gene expression values in the range -100 to 100 indicate the highly dense profiles of the co regulated genes having little or no fluctuations under the selected conditions of the bicluster. However, there also exist a few genes having large expression values. This is perhaps because of the presence of a large number of missing values (12.3%) that are replaced by random numbers between -800 and 800, some of which remain in the biclusters without violating the homogeneity constraint. Sometimes this can also occur when a few genes having large variation in their expression values get included while continuing to satisfy the homogeneity constraint of the bicluster. Although it is possible to deterministically eliminate these highly fluctuating genes.

26

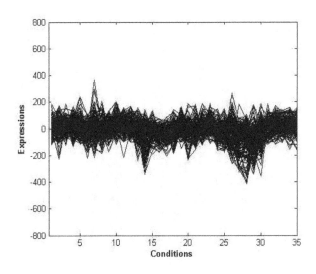

Figure 3.4. Gene expression profile of the largest bicluster on Lymphoma data

3.2.4   Biological Relevance

With the intention of evaluating the biological relevance of CS algorithm, the results of the proposed method are compared with CC, ISA, Bimax, OPSM and BiMine on yeast cell-cycle dataset from Ayadi et al. (2009) by using web-tool of FuncAssociate. The FuncAssociate computes the adjusted significance scores for each bicluster. Indeed, the adjusted significance scores assess genes in each bicluster by computing adjusted p-values, which indicates how well they match with the different GO categories. Note that a smaller p-value, close to 0, is indicative of a better match. Figure 3.5 represents the different values of significant scores p-value for each algorithm over the percentage of total extracted biclusters. In fact with CS, 100% of tested biclusters have p-value = 5% and 1%. Finally, 65% of extracted biclusters with CS have p-value = 0.001%, while those of BiMine have 51%. Note that CS performs well for all p-values compared to CC, ISA, Bimax, OPSM and BiMine.

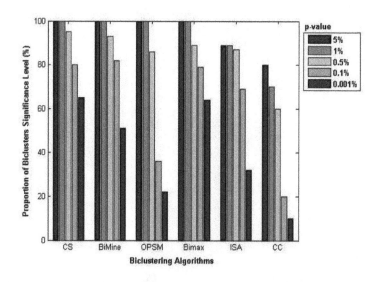

Figure 3.5 Proportions of biclusters significantly enriched by GO annotations on yeast cell-cycle.

3.2.5 Biological Annotation for Yeast cell cycle using GOTermFinder Toolbox

Table 3.4 lists the significant shared GO terms (or parent of GO terms) used to describe the set of genes in each bicluster for the process, function and component ontologies. For example, to the bicluster BC_1, the genes are mainly involved in translation process, structural constituent of ribosome activity and cytosolic ribosome component. The tuple ($n=78$, $p=3.15\times10^{-95}$) represents that out of 184 genes in bicluster BC_1, 78 genes belong to in cytoplasmic translation process, and the statistical significance is given by the p-value of $p=3.15\times10^{-95}$. Next, the tuple ($n=69$, $p=2.52\times10^{-68}$) represents that out of 184 genes in bicluster BC_1, 69 genes belong to structural constituent of ribosome activity function, and the statistical significance is given by the p-value of $p=2.52\times10^{-68}$. Finally the genes 63 out of 184 belong to component of cytosolic ribosome and the corresponding p-value is $p=8.41\times10^{-73}$.

Bicluster	No. of. Genes	Process	Function	Component
BC$_1$	184	cytoplasmic translation (n=78, p=3.15×10^{-95})	structural constituent of ribosome (n=69, p=2.52×10^{-68})	cytosolic ribosome (n=63, p=8.41×10^{-73})
		ribosome biogenesis (n=83, p=6.27×10^{-54})	structural molecule (n=73, p=1.08×10^{-45})	cytosolic part (n=79, p=6.17×10^{-45})
		cellular metabolic process (n=156, p=4.63×10^{-28})	RNA binding (n=34, p=3.11×10^{-29})	organelle part (n=79, p=1.45×10^{-21})

Table 3.4. Significant GO terms for three biclusters on yeast cell data

In Figure 3.6 depicts the significant GO terms (or parents of GO terms) for a set of 20 genes along with their p-values, with the significance being indicated in terms of the grayness displayed. It shows the branching of a generalized molecular function into sub-functions like structural molecule activity and binding etc., which are then clustered gene-wise to produce the final result. Moreover out of 20 genes, the 8 genes (RPS16B, RPP1B, RPL35B, RPL35A, RPL4B, RPS11A, RPS13, RPP2B) are involved in structural constituent of ribosome activity and 2 genes (RPP2B, RPP1B) are in protein kinase activator activity. Further the corresponding p-value is very small (p= 1.39×10^{-6} & p= 0.00076) which shows that there is very less probability to obtain the gene cluster in random. Those result means that the proposed CS biclustering approach can find biologically meaningful biclusters.

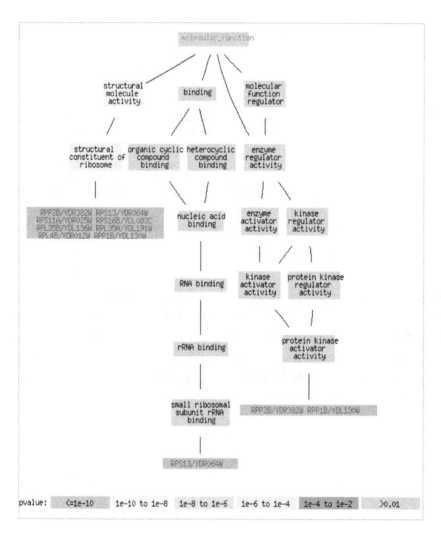

Figure 3.6. Gene Ontology biological functions of yeast cell cycle data with (20 genes)

3.4   SUMMARY

In this work CS algorithm for biclustering microarray gene expression data is proposed. It focuses on finding coherent bicluster with lower MSR and higher row variance. The CS preserves the balanced exploitation and exploration in the solution of the search space. A qualitative measure of the formed biclusters of results are provided on two benchmark gene expression datasets to demonstrate the effectiveness of the proposed method. Biological validation of the selected genes within the biclusters has been provided by publicly available GO consortium. The patterns present a significant biological relevance in terms of related biological processes, components and molecular functions in a species-independent manner. Thus the CS algorithm finds biologically relevant and statistically significant biclusters in microarray gene expression data.

REFERENCES

1. D.J. Lockhart, and E.A. Winzeler, "Genomics, gene expression and DNA arrays," Nature, Vol. 405, pp. 827-836, 2000.

2. K.S. Pollard, and M.J. Van Der Laan, "Statistical Inference for Simultaneous Clustering of Gene Expression Data", Mathematical Biosciences, Vol. 176, No. 1, pp 99-121, 2002.

3. A.Mukhopadhyay , U. Maulik and S. Bandyopadhyay, "Finding multiple coherent biclusters in microarray data using varible string length multiobjective genetic algorithm", IEEE Transactions on Information Technology in Biomedicine, Vol. 13, No. 6, pp. 969-975, 2009.

4. S.C. Madeira and A.L. Oliveira, "Biclustering algorithms for biological data analysis: A survey," IEEE/ACM Transactions on Computational Biology and Bioinformatics, Vol. 1, No. 1 pp. 24 – 45, 2004.

5. Y. Cheng and G. M. Church "Biclustering of expression data", In Proceedings of the Eighth International Conference on Intelligent Systems for Molecular Biology, pp. 93–103. AAAI Press, 2000.

6. A.Tanay, R. Sharan, and R. Shamir, "Discovering statistically significant biclusters in gene expression data," Bioinformatics, Vol. 18, pp. 136-144, 2002.

7. J. A. Hartigan, "Direct clustering of a data matrix", Journal of the American Statistical Association, Vol. 67, No. 337, pp. 123–129, 1972.

8. A. Prelic, S. Bleuler, P. Zimmermann, P. Buhlmann, W. Gruissem, L. Hennig, L. Thiele, and E. Zitzler, "A systematic comparison and evaluation of biclustering methods for gene expression data", Bioinformatics, Vol. 22, No. 9, pp. 1122–1129, 2006.

9. H. Zhaoa, A.W. Liewb, X. Xie and H. Yan, "A new geometric biclusteringe algorithm based on the Hough transform for analysis of large-scale microarray data", Journal of Theoritical Biology, Vol. 251, pp. 264-274, 2008.

10. W.H. Yang, D.Q. Dai, H. and Yan H, "Finding correlated biclusters from gene expression data", IEEE Transactions on Knowledge and Data Engineering, Vol. 23, pp. 568-584, 2011.

11. A. Ben-Dor, B. Chor, R. Karp, and Z. Yakhini, "Discovering local structure in gene expression data: The order-preserving submatrix problem," Journal of Computational Biology, Vol. 10, No. 4, pp. 373-384, 2003.

12. S. Bergmann, J. Ihmels, and N. Barkai. "Iterative signature algorithm for the analysis of large-scale gene expression data," Physics Review E, Vol. 67, pp. 1-18, 2003.

13. J. Yang, H. Wang, W. Wang, and P. Yu, "Enhanced biclustering on expression data", In Proceedings of the 3rd IEEE Symposium on BioInformatics and BioEngineering, Washington, DC, USA, pp. 321-327, 2003.

14. X. Liu, and L. Wang, "Computing the maximum similarity bi-clusters of gene expression data," Bioinformatics, Vol. 23, No. 1, pp. 50-56, 2007.

15. P. DiMaggio, S. McAllister, C. Floudas, X. Feng, J. Rabinowitz, and H. Rabitz, "Biclustering via optimal re-ordering of data matrices in systems biology: rigorous methods and comparative studies," Bioinformatis, Vol. 9, No. 1, pp. 458-467, 2008.

16. F. Angiulli, E. Cesario, and C. Pizzuti, "Random walk biclustering for microarray data", Journal of Information Sciences, Vol. 178, No. 6, pp. 1479–1497, 2008.

17. G. Li, Q. Ma, H. Tang, A.H. Paterson, and Y. Xu, "Qubic: a qualitative biclustering algorithm for analyses of gene expression data", Nucleic acids research, Vol. 37, No. 15, e101. doi: 10.1093/nar/gkp491, 2009.

18. W. Ayadi, M. Elloumi, and J.K. Hao, "Bicfinder: a biclustering algorithm for microarray data analysis. Knowledge and Information Systems ", Vol. 30, No. 2, pp 341-358, 2009

19. L. Zhao, M. Zaki, "Microcluster: Efficient deterministic biclustering of microarray data", IEEE Intelligent Systems, Vol. 20, No. 6, pp. 40-49, 2005.

20. W. Ayadi, M. Elloumi, and J. K. Hao, "A biclustering algorithm based on a bicluster enumeration tree : Application to DNA microarray data", BioData Mining, Vol. 2, No. 9, 2009.

21. W. Ayadi, M. Elloumi, and J. K. Hao, "BiMine+: an efficient algorithm for discovering relevant biclusters of DNA microarray data", Knowledge-Based Systems, Vol. 35, pp. 224-234, 2012.

22. S. Roy, D.K. Bhattacharyya, and J.K. Kalita, "CoBi: Pattern Based Co-Regulated Biclustering of Gene Expression Data," Pattern Recognition Letter, Vol. 34, No. 14, pp. 1669-1678, 2013.

23. K. Bryan, P. Cunningham, and N. Bolshakova, "Application of simulated annealing to the biclustering of gene expression data", IEEE Transactions on Information Technology on Biomedicine, Vol. 10, No. 3, pp. 519–525, 2006.

24. J. Liu, Z. Li, X. Hu , Y. Chen, "Biclustering of microarray data with mospo based on crowding distance", Bioinformatics, Vol. 10(Suppl 4):S9, 2009.

25. W. Ayadi, M. Elloumi, and J. K. Hao, "Pattern-driven neighborhood search for biclustering of microarray data", BMC Genomics, Vol. 13(Suppl 3):S6, 2012.

26. S. Bleuler, A. Prelic, and E. Zitzler, "An EA framework for biclustering of geneexpression data", In Proceedings of Congress on Evolutionary Computation, pp. 166–173, 2004.

27. F. Divina, and J.S. Aguilar-Ruiz, "Biclustering of expression data with evolutionary computation," IEEE Transations Knowlede and Data Engineering, Vol. 18, No. 5, 2006, pp. 590-602.

28. S. Mitra, and H. Banka. "Multi-objective evolutionary biclustering of gene expression data," Pattern Recognition Letter, Vol. 39, No. 12, pp. 2464-2477, 2006.

29. Liu Feng, Zhou Huaibei, Liu Juan. "Biclustering of Gene Expression Data Using EDA-GA Hybrid". Evolutionary Computation, 2006. CEC 2006. IEEE Congress on 16-21 July pp.1598-1602, 2006.

30. C. A. Gallo, J. A. Carballido, and I. Ponzoni, "Microarray biclustering: A novel memetic approach based on the pisa platform", In Proceedings of the 7th European Conference on Evolutionary Computation, Machine Learning and Data Mining in Bioinformatics, 2009, pp. 44–55, Berlin, Heidelberg, 2009.

31. Q. Huang, D. Tao, X. Li, and A.W.C. Liew, "Parallelized evolutionary learning for detection of biclusters in gene expression data," IEEE/ACM Transaction Computatonal Biology and Bioinformatics, Vol. 9, No. 1, pp. 560-570, 2012.

32. O. Maatouk, W. Ayadi, H. Bouziri and B. Duval, "Evolutionary Algorithm Based on New Crossover for the Biclustering of Gene Expression Data", Proceedings of the Pattern Recognition in Bioinformatics: Nineth International Conference on IAPR, Stockholm, Sweden, pp. 48-59, 2014.

33. X. S. Yang, Nature-Inspired Metaheuristic Algorithms, 2nd edition, Luniver Press, 2010

34. X.S. Yang, and S. Deb, "Cuckoo search via Levy flights", Proceedings of World Congress on Nature & Biologically Inspired Computing, pp. 210 – 214, 2009.

35. R. Dawkins, The Selfish Gene , 30th ed., Oxford University Press, New York,1989.

YOUR KNOWLEDGE HAS VALUE